CLASSICAL SOLOS
FOR
BARITONE
B.C.

15 Easy Solos for Contest and Performance

Arranged by Philip Sparke

ONLINE MEDIA INCLUDED
Audio Recordings
Printable Piano Accompaniments

PLAYBACK+
Speed • Pitch • Balance • Loop

To access recordings and PDF accompaniments visit:
www.halleonard.com/mylibrary

Enter Code
1649-2348-2919-8326

ISBN 978-1-70516-745-8

Copyright © 2011 by HAL LEONARD CORPORATION
International Copyright Secured   All Rights Reserved

Visit Hal Leonard Online at
www.halleonard.com

World headquarters, contact:
Hal Leonard
7777 West Bluemound Road
Milwaukee, WI 53213
Email: info@halleonard.com

In Europe, contact:
Hal Leonard Europe Limited
1 Red Place
London, W1K 6PL
Email: info@halleonardeurope.com

In Australia, contact:
Hal Leonard Australia Pty. Ltd.
4 Lentara Court
Cheltenham, Victoria, 3192 Australia
Email: info@halleonard.com.au

WALTZ

BARITONE B.C.

MORITZ VOGEL
Arranged by PHILIP SPARKE

00870098

CHORALE

Now praise, my soul, the Lord

BARITONE B.C.

JOHANN SEBASTIAN BACH
Arranged by PHILIP SPARKE

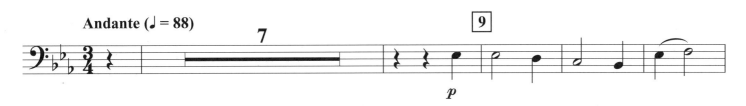

00870098

4

HUMMING SONG
from *Album for the Young*

BARITONE B.C.

ROBERT SCHUMANN
Arranged by PHILIP SPARKE

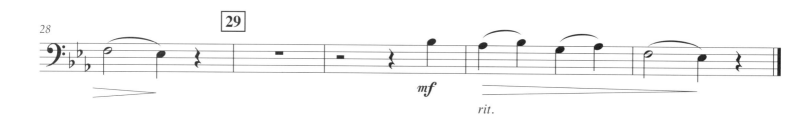

00870098

GYMNOPÉDIE NO. 1

BARITONE B.C.

ERIK SATIE
Arranged by PHILIP SPARKE

I'M CALLED LITTLE BUTTERCUP

from *HMS Pinafore*

BARITONE B.C.

SIR ARTHUR SULLIVAN
Arranged by PHILIP SPARKE

STUDY
Op. 37, No. 3

BARITONE B.C.

HENRY LEMOINE
Arranged by PHILIP SPARKE

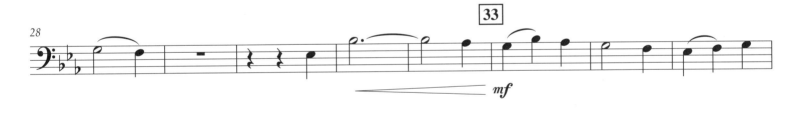

00870098

MINUET
(Z. 649)

BARITONE B.C.

HENRY PURCELL
Arranged by PHILIP SPARKE

Allegro (♩ = 152)

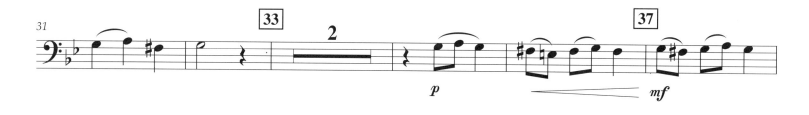

00870098

THEME AND VARIATION

from *Sonatina No. 3*

BARITONE B.C.

THOMAS ATTWOOD
Arranged by PHILIP SPARKE

00870098

NORTHERN SONG

from *Album for the Young*

BARITONE B.C.

ROBERT SCHUMANN
Arranged by PHILIP SPARKE

TWO GERMAN DANCES

from *Twelve German Dances, D. 420*

BARITONE B.C.

FRANZ SCHUBERT
Arranged by PHILIP SPARKE

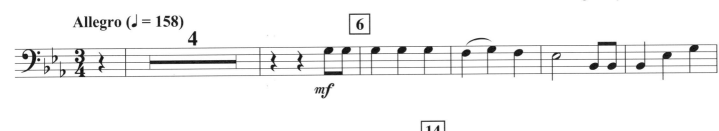

WATCHMAN'S SONG

from *Lyric Pieces, Op. 12*

BARITONE B.C.

EDVARD GRIEG
Arranged by PHILIP SPARKE

GAVOTTE

BARITONE B.C.

JAN LADISLAV DUSSEK
Arranged by PHILIP SPARKE

00870098

VIEN QUÀ, DORINA BELLA

BARITONE B.C.

ANTONIO BIANCHI
Transcribed by **C. M. von WEBER**
Arranged by PHILIP SPARKE

00870098

MINUET

from *Notebook for Anna Magdalena Bach*

BARITONE B.C.

Attributed to **CHRISTIAN PETZOLD**
Arranged by PHILIP SPARKE

00870098

THE PRINCE OF DENMARK'S MARCH

from *Choice Lessons for the Harpsichord or Spinet*

BARITONE B.C.

JEREMIAH CLARKE
Arranged by PHILIP SPARKE